HORRID
HE...
JOKE...

Francesca Simon spent her childhood on the beach in California, and then went to Yale and Oxford Universities to study medieval history and literature. She now lives in London with her English husband and their son. When she is not writing books she is doing theatre and restaurant reviews or chasing after her Tibetan Spaniel, Shanti.

Also by Francesca Simon

Horrid Henry
Horrid Henry and the Secret Club
Horrid Henry Tricks the Tooth Fairy
Horrid Henry's Nits
Horrid Henry Gets Rich Quick
Horrid Henry's Haunted House
Horrid Henry and the Mummy's Curse
Horrid Henry's Revenge
Horrid Henry and the Bogey Babysitter
Horrid Henry's Stinkbomb
Horrid Henry's Underpants

Helping Hercules

and for younger readers

Don't be Horrid, Henry
Illustrated by Kevin McAleenan

HORRID HENRY'S JOKE BOOK

Illustrated by Tony Ross

Dolphin Paperbacks

To the children of Yerbury Primary School, who told Henry such brilliant jokes

First published in Great Britain in 2004
by Dolphin paperbacks
an imprint of Orion Children's Books
a division of the Orion Publishing Group Ltd
Orion House
5 Upper St Martin's Lane
London WC2H 9EA

This collection copyright © Francesca Simon 2004
Illustrations copyright © Tony Ross 2004

The moral rights of the author and
illustrator have been asserted.

All rights reserved. No part of this publication may be
reproduced, stored in a retrieval system, or transmitted,
in any form or by any means, electronic, mechanical,
photocopying, recording or otherwise, without the prior
permission of Orion Children's Books.

A catalogue record for this book
is available from the British Library

Printed in Great Britain
by Clays Ltd, St Ives plc

ISBN 1 84255 160 4

CONTENTS

Warning!

Do not read this joke book if:
- ☠ Your name is Prissy Polly
- ☠ You're a goody-goody, ugly toad, tattle-tale
- ☠ You watch Nellie's Nursery on TV

These jokes are horrid. These jokes are guaranteed to make horrible little brothers feel sick and parents run screaming from the room. These jokes are so rude and so gross that —

'Oy! Peter! Stop reading right now. I said, put down my book - or else. These gross out jokes are

not for little toads!'

'Muuum! Henry's being mean to me!'

'Don't be horrid, Henry. Let Peter read your jokes.'

'NO!'

MUMMY'S CURSE JOKES

Why didn't the skeleton and the monster fight? The skeleton didn't have the guts.

Why was the Egyptian boy upset? His daddy was a mummy.

During which age did mummies live?
The Band-age.

*What does a monster mummy say to her kids
at lunch?*
Don't talk with someone in your mouth.

*What did the metal monster want written
on his gravestone?*
Rust in piece.

What pets does Dracula own?
A bloodhound and a
ghoulfish.

What is sung in the vampire production of Abba hits?
Fang you for the music.

Who works in monster hospitals?
A skeleton staff.

What feature do witches love having on their computers?
A spell checker.

What should you do after shaking hands with a monster?
Count your fingers.

When a vampire drinks too much, what does it get?
A fangover.

What did the vampire crawling through the desert say?
'Blood! Blood!'

What do vampires cross the sea in?
Blood vessels.

Which monster ate the three bears' porridge?
Ghouldilocks.

What do you call a ghostly teddy bear?
Winnie the OOOOOHhhhhhhh.

What haircut do monsters like?
Deadlocks.

What did the pirate get when he hit the skeleton?
A skull and very cross bones.

Why didn't the skeleton go to the party?
He had nobody to go with.

Where do skeletons swim?
The Dead Sea.

BOY: Mummy, Mummy, Ralph just called me a werewolf.
MUM: Shut up and comb your face.

Why are zombies never lonely?
They can always dig up a few friends.

What do you get if a huge, hairy monster
steps on Batman and Robin?
Flatman and Ribbon

HANGMAN: Do you have a last
  request?
PRISONER: Yes, can I sing a song?
HANGMAN: All right. Just one.
PRISONER: Ten million green bottles,
  standing on a wall . . .

Why is the letter V like a monster?
It comes after U.

What did the monster say to his daughter?
'You're the apple of my eye eye eye eye.'

What is a monster's favourite game?
Hide and shriek.

What should you say if you meet a ghost?
How do you boo?

What do little ghosts drink?
Evaporated milk.

When do ghosts usually appear?
Just before someone screams.

What would you find on a haunted beach?
A sandwitch.

*What do short-
sighted ghosts
wear?*
Spooktacles.

Why did the mummy have no friends?
He was too wrapped up in himself.

Where do ghosts go on holiday?
Death Valley.

GRISLY GRUB JOKES

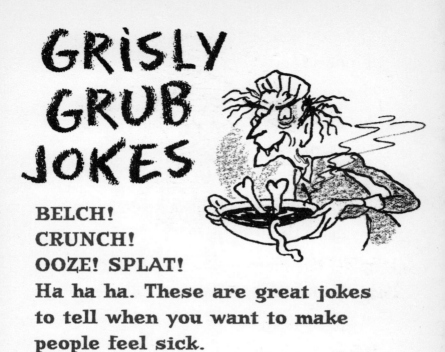

**BELCH!
CRUNCH!
OOZE! SPLAT!**
Ha ha ha. These are great jokes
to tell when you want to make
people feel sick.

VAMPIRE TO SON: You're late. We had
guests for dinner. They were delicious!

What do cannibals like for breakfast?
Buttered host.

What does Dracula like for breakfast?
Ready neck.

What do monsters call knights in armour?
Tinned food.

What do monsters make with cars?
Traffic jam.

What do cannibals play at parties?
Swallow the leader.

What does a sea-monster eat for dinner?
Fish and ships.

How do monsters have their eggs?
Terrifried.

What's the difference between school dinners and slugs?
School dinners come on plates.

What do you call someone who puts poison on their breakfast?
A cereal killer.

What do mermaids have on toast?
Mermalade.

Why did the man drown in his muesli?
He was pulled under by a strong currant.

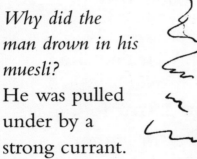

What's yellow and dangerous?
Shark-infested custard.

What do you get if you cross an egg with a barrel of gunpowder?
A boom-meringue.

Waiter! Waiter! Your thumb is in my soup.
Don't worry. It's not hot.

Waiter! Waiter! This egg is bad.
Don't blame me, I only laid the table.

Waiter! Waiter! There's a fly in my soup.
I'm sorry, sir, the dog must have missed it.

HENRY: Why is your thumb on my
    sandwich?
DEMON DINNER LADY: To stop it
    falling on the floor again.

*What's worse than finding a
caterpillar in your apple?*
Finding half a caterpillar
in your apple.

Why don't cannibals eat clowns?
Because they taste funny.

What do French pupils say after finishing school dinners?
Mercy.

What happened to the butcher who backed into a meat grinder?
He got a little behind in his work.

HENRY: What's yellow, brown and hairy?
PETER: I don't know.
HENRY: Cheese on toast stuck to the carpet.

What do cannibals do at weddings?
Toast the bride and groom.

What do you give a cannibal who's late for dinner?
The cold shoulder.

What's yellow, flat and flies around the kitchen?
An unidentified flying omelette.

What's the worst thing you'll find in a school canteen?
The food.

MISS BATTLE-AXE: Henry, how many bones have you got in your body?

HENRY: It feels like 4,000. I had fish for school dinner.

GROSS-OUT JOKES

'Out of my way, worm! These jokes are much too gross for you!'

What happens when a baby eats Rice Krispies?
It goes snap, crackle and poop.

Why is your mouth all fluffy?
My mum hoovered up my toffee.

What do you get if you sit under a cow?
A pat on the head.

What monster do you get at the end of your finger?
A bogey monster.

Waiter! Waiter! There's a fly in my soup.
Quiet or everyone will want one.

What's green and hangs from trees?
Giraffe snot.

What do you give sea-sick elephants?
Plenty of room.

What's an ig?
An Eskimo's house without a toilet.

What's an insect's best chat-up line?
'Is this stool taken?'

What goes ha-ha-bonk?
A man laughing his head
off.

*Why did the sand
scream?*
The sea weed.

What do you do when your nose goes on strike?
Picket.

How do you make a tissue dance?
Put a little boogie in it.

Knock knock.
Who's there?
Alec.
Alec who?
Alec to pick my nose.

Knock knock.
Who's there?
Ahab.
Ahab who?
Ahab to go to
the loo.

What's brown and sticky?
A brown stick.

BOGEY BABYSITTER JOKES

Warning! Make sure you can make a quick getaway if you tell a rabid babysitter any of these jokes. Believe me, I know.

HENRY: Rebecca, you remind me of a movie star.

RABID REBECCA: Oooh. Which one?

HENRY: The Incredible Hulk.

RABID REBECCA: I always speak my mind.

HENRY: I'm surprised you have so much to say then.

RABID REBECCA: Whenever I'm down in the dumps, I buy myself a new T-shirt.

HENRY: So *that's* where you get them.

HENRY: Why do I have to go to bed?

REBECCA: Because the bed won't come to you.

REBECCA: How long can someone live without a brain?

HENRY: How old are you?

Did you hear about the babysitter who accidentally plugged her electric blanket into the toaster?

She spent the night popping out of bed.

Nah nah ne nah nah

TERMINATOR GLADIATOR JOKES

If you want to make your mean, horrible parents really scream, just tell them one of these jokes.

What do you call a sheep with a machine gun?
Lambo.

What's got four legs and an arm?
A Rottweiler.

What do you call a budgie that's been run over by a lawn mower?
Shredded tweet.

What did the fly say as it hit the windscreen?
That's me all over.

What's the last thing that goes through a wasp's mind when it hits a windscreen?
Its sting.

What's green and red and goes round and round?
A frog in a blender.

What do you call a cow with no legs?
Ground beef.

Why did the hedgehog cross the road?
To see his flatmate.

Did you hear about the man who had a dog with no legs?
He took it for a drag every day.

How do you kill a circus?
Go for the juggler.

UNDERPANTS JOKES

Boy oh boy! Jokes do not get more horrid than these.

What's hairy, scary and wears its knickers on its head?
The Underwere-wolf.

What are two robbers called?
A pair of nickers.

Why do werewolves have holes in their underpants?
So furry tails can come true.

What gushes out of the ground shouting,
'Knickers, knickers'?
Crude oil.

What gushes out of the ground shouting,
'Underwear, underwear'?
Refined oil.

What hangs out your underpants?
Your mum.

Why did the golfer
wear two pairs of
pants?
In case he
got a hole
in one.

What's the best way to make pants last?
Make vests first.

Knock knock.
Who's there?
Nicholas.
Nicholas who?
Nicholas girls shouldn't climb trees.

What goes 300mph on a washing line?
Honda pants.

*What do you get if you pull your underwear
up to your neck?*
A chest of drawers.

MINI MINNIE: Do you know how old Miss Battle-Axe is?

LISPING LILLY: No, but I know how to find out. Take off her knickers!

MINI MINNIE: Take off her knickers! How will that tell us?

LISPING LILLY: 'Well, in my knickers it says, '3 to 5 years'.

STINK BOMBS

Hold your nose for these stinkers!

What did the skunk say when the wind blew in the opposite direction?
It's all coming back to me now.

What do you get if you cross a bear with a skunk?
Winnie the Poo.

How do you stop someone who's been working out in the gym on a hot day from smelling?
Put a peg on his nose.

Why do giraffes have long necks?
Their feet smell.

What did one burp say to the other?
Let's be stinkers and
sneak out the other
end.
**(Ralph's
favourite
joke)**

*What happens when you play table
tennis with a rotten egg?*
First it goes ping, then it goes pong.

What's brown and sits on a piano stool?
Beethoven's last movement.

*What do you get if you cross a skunk with a
cuckoo?*
A bird that stinks and doesn't give a hoot.

What do you call a flying skunk?
A smellicopter.

What's the hairiest, smelliest thing on earth
(besides Peter)*?*
King Pong.

DOCTOR DETTOL JOKES

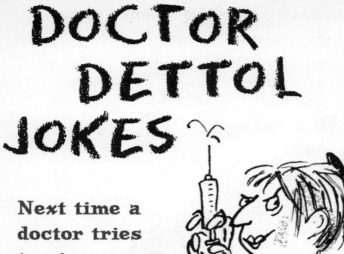

Next time a doctor tries to give you an injection, distract her with a few of these goodies.

Doctor, Doctor, I think I'm a pair of curtains.
Well, pull yourself together.

Did you hear about the man who swallowed some Christmas decorations?
He got tinselitis.

Doctor, Doctor, what's a good cure for snake bites?
Stop biting so many snakes.

What did the vampire doctor say to his patients?
Necks please.

Doctor, Doctor, can you give me something for wind?
Sure, take this kite.

When is the best time to visit the dentist?
Tooth-hurty.

Doctor, Doctor, people keep ignoring me.
Who said that?

What is the most common illness in China?
Kung flu.

Doctor, Doctor, you have to help me out.
Which way did you come in?

Doctor, Doctor, I feel as if I'm getting smaller.
You'll just have to be a little patient.

Doctor, Doctor, there's something wrong with my tummy.
Keep your jumper on and nobody will notice.

A girl walks into the doctor's office. She has a banana in her left ear and a carrot in her right. There's a piece of celery in one nostril and a small potato in the other.

'Doctor, I feel terrible,' she says.

'Well, your problem is obvious,' says the doctor. 'You're clearly not eating properly.'

Doctor Doctor, I keep thinking I'm a bell. Take this medicine and, if it doesn't work, give me a ring.

Doctor, Doctor, I feel like a biscuit.
You must be crackers.

Doctor, Doctor, I've just swallowed a roll of film.
Sit in the sunshine and hope that nothing develops.

Doctor, Doctor, I think I need glasses.
You certainly do, sir. This is a flower shop.

Doctor, Doctor, I keep seeing insects spinning.
Don't worry. It's just a bug that's going round.

DiZZY DAVE'S DiNOSAUR JOKES

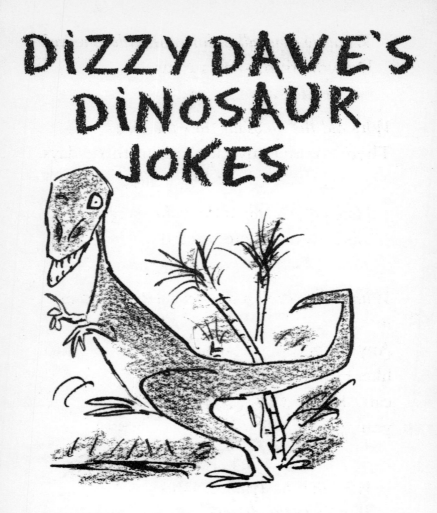

Dave paid me £1, so I let him add a few dinosaur jokes to my book.

What do you call a dinosaur with one eye?
Do-you-think-he-saur-us.

Why did the dinosaur cross the road?
There weren't any chickens in those days.

How do you stop a dinosaur charging?
Take away his credit card.

*What do you call a dinosaur with a banana
in each ear?*
Anything you
like. He
can't hear
you.

*Why did the Tyrannosaurus
Rex go to the doctor?*
He had a dino-sore.

What do you get when dinosaurs crash their cars?
Tyrannosaurus wrecks.

What do you call it when a Tyrannosaurus Rex gets the ball into the back of the net?
A dino-score.

What do you get when you cross a Tyrannosaurus Rex with fireworks?
Dino-mite.

What was the scariest prehistoric animal?
The Terror-dactyl.

What did dinosaurs have that no other animals ever had?
Baby dinosaurs.

What do you call a Tyrannosaurus Rex that sleeps all day?
A dino-snore.

Why do Tyrannosaurus Rex like to eat snowmen?
They melt in their mouths.

What's huge and bumps into mountains?
A dinosaur playing blind man's buff.

What do you call a dinosaur with no head?
A Tyrannosaurus Nex.

What do you get if you cross a dinosaur with a pig?
Jurassic Pork.

How can you tell if a dinosaur is a vegetarian?
Lie down on a plate.

Why did the Tyrannosaurus Rex cross the road?
So he could eat the chickens on the other side.

MOODY MARGARET KNOCKS SOUR SUSAN JOKES

The only good thing about living next door to Moody Margaret is that she knows some good jokes. There's just one problem . . .

MARGARET: Knock Knock.
SUSAN: Who's there?
MARGARET: Little old lady.
SUSAN: Little old lady who?
MARGARET (yodelling): Little old lady ooooh.

MARGARET: Knock Knock.
SUSAN: Who's there?
MARGARET: Abyssinia.
SUSAN: Abyssinia who?
MARGARET: Abyssinia when I get back.

MARGARET: Knock Knock.
SUSAN: Who's there?
MARGARET: Canoe.
SUSAN: Canoe who?
MARGARET: Canoe open the door? It's cold out here.

MARGARET: Knock Knock.
SUSAN: Who's there?
MARGARET: Bella.
SUSAN: Bella who?
MARGARET: Bella bottom trousers.

MARGARET:
Knock Knock.
SUSAN: Who's there?
MARGARET: Dishes.
SUSAN: Dishes who?
MARGARET: Dishes your friend. Let me in.

MARGARET: Knock knock.
SUSAN: Who's there?
MARGARET: Lettuce.
SUSAN: Lettuce who?
MARGARET: Lettuce in, it's raining.

MARGARET: Knock knock.

SUSAN: Who's there?

MARGARET: Sorry.

SUSAN: Sorry who?

MARGARET: Sorry, wrong door.

MARGARET: Knock knock.

SUSAN: Who's there?

MARGARET: Boo.

SUSAN: Boo who?

MARGARET: Don't cry, it's only a joke.

MARGARET: Knock knock.

SUSAN: Who's there?

MARGARET: Abby.

SUSAN: Abby who?

MARGARET: Abby stung me on the bottom.

MARGARET: Knock knock.

SUSAN: Who's there?

MARGARET: Nun.

SUSAN: Nun who?

MARGARET: Nun of your business.

MARGARET: Knock knock.

SUSAN: Who's there?

MARGARET: Germaine.

SUSAN: Germaine who?

MARGARET: Germaine you don't recognise me?

MARGARET: Knock knock.

SUSAN: Who's there?

MARGARET: Ron.

SUSAN: Ron who?

MARGARET: Ron as fast as you can!

MARGARET: Knock knock.

SUSAN: Who's there?

MARGARET: Ada.

SUSAN: Ada who?

MARGARET: Ada lot of breakfast and
I'm stuffed.

MARGARET: Knock knock.

SUSAN: Who's there?

MARGARET: Cows go.

SUSAN: Cows go who?

MARGARET: No they don't,
they go moo.

MARGARET: Knock knock.

SUSAN: Who's there?

MARGARET: Adjust.

SUSAN: Adjust who?

MARGARET: Adjust made a mess on
the floor.

I couldn't steal any more of their
jokes because . . . Aarrrggghhh!
I'm getting out of here!

'How come you always get to go
first?' said Susan sourly.

'Because you can't tell jokes
and I can,' said Margaret.

'I can too tell
jokes!'

'Can't!'

'Can!'

SLAP!

SLAP!

BEEFY BERT'S BEASTLY JOKES

HENRY: Bert, why did the chicken cross the road?

BERT: I dunno.

HENRY: There's no point telling you jokes, Bert! Why do you always answer, 'I dunno'?

BERT: I dunno.

What do you get if you cross a centipede with a parrot?
A walkie-talkie.

What do you call a sheep with no legs?
A cloud.

Why do ducks have webbed feet?
To stamp out forest fires.

Why do elephants have big, flat feet?
To stamp out flaming ducks.

What goes 99-clonk, 99-clonk, 99-clonk?
A centipede with a wooden leg.

How do you hire a horse?
Put a brick under each hoof.

What's worse than an alligator with toothache?
A centipede with athlete's foot.

How do you know which end of a worm is its head?
Tickle it and see which end smiles.

What has 50 legs but can't walk?
Half a centipede.

What has four wheels and flies?
A rubbish bin.

What did the slug say as he slipped down the wall?
How slime flies.

Why did the turkey cross the road?
It was the chicken's day off.

How do you know when there's an elephant under your bed?
Your nose touches the ceiling.

What's grey and squirts jam at you?
A mouse eating a doughnut.

What did the teddy bear say when he was offered dessert?
No thanks, I'm stuffed.

How does an elephant get up a tree?
Sits on an acorn and waits for it to grow.

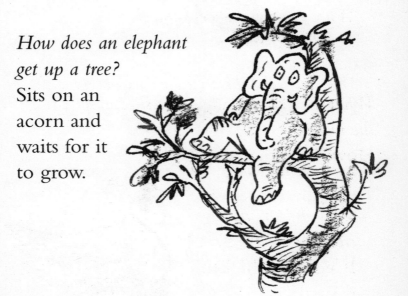

How does an elephant get down from a tree?
Sits on a leaf and waits for it to fall.

What's black and white and red all over?
A zebra in a phone box.

Where do frogs keep their money?
In riverbanks.

How long should a giraffe's legs be?
Long enough to touch the ground.

What's a chicken's favourite TV programme?
The feather forecast.

Why do mice need oiling?
They squeak.

What bird is always out of breath?
A puffin.

What do you call a carton of ducks?
A box of quackers.

What's a frog's favourite drink?
Croak-a-Cola.

What do you call a crocodile at the North Pole?
Lost.

How do you stop moles digging up the garden?
Hide their shovels.

What do you call a fly with no wings?
A walk.

An elephant is walking through the jungle when he sees a turtle sitting by a log.

'Hey,' says the elephant, 'you're the turtle that bit me 57 years ago.'

'How on earth do you remember that?' asks the turtle.

'Easy,' says the elephant, 'I've got turtle recall.'

AEROBIC AL'S SPORTS JOKES

I hate PE! I hate Sports Day, too, unless of course I win everything. But Al promised to pick me ahead of Margaret for football today if I let him put some jokes in my book. It'll be worth it just to see the look on Margaret's grumpy, misery-gut face!

Why is Cinderella bad at football?
She has a pumpkin as her coach.

Why was Cinderella knocked out of the football team?
She kept running away from the ball.

What did one earwig say to the other earwig as they fell out of a tree?
Earwig go, earwig go, earwig go.

Where do footballers dance?
At a football.

Why don't grasshoppers go to football games?
They prefer cricket matches.

What football team
does King Kong support?
Aston Gorilla.

Why were the flies playing
football in a saucer?
They were practising for
the cup.

What's an insect's favourite game?
Cricket.

Why couldn't the car play football?
It had only one boot.

Why did the basketball player go to the doctor?
To get more shots.

What is a goal-keeper's favourite snack?
Beans on post.

How did the basketball court get wet?
The players dribbled all over it.

What do you call a cat that plays football?
Puss in boots.

Why do elephants have grey trunks?
They're all on the same swimming team.

How did the football pitch become a triangle?
Somebody took a corner.

Why should Sports Days never be held in the jungle?
There are too many cheetahs.

Why wasn't the footballer invited to dinner?
He dribbled too much.

Why didn't the dog like swimming?
It was a boxer.

What part of a swimming pool is never the same?
The changing rooms.

Where do old bowling balls end up?
The gutter.

*What happened when two balls of string had
a race?*
It ended in a tie.

What's Aerobic Al's favourite subject in school?
Jog-graphy.

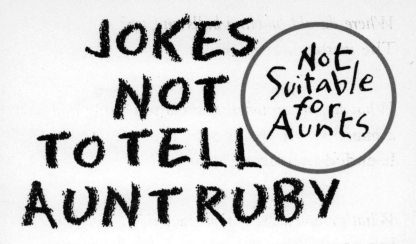

JOKES NOT TO TELL AUNT RUBY

Not Suitable for Aunts

MUM: Henry! I've just had the strangest call from Aunt Ruby. . .
HENRY: Hide!

What do you call an aunt on the toilet?
Lou Lou.

What do you call an aunt who falls off the toilet?
Lou Roll.

Why do you put your aunt in the fridge?
To make Auntie-freeze.

Has your aunt caught up with you yet?
No, but when she does I'm going to need a lot of Auntie-septic.

How do you make anti-freeze?
Hide her nightie.

How can you tell if Aunt Ruby's been to visit?
She's still in the house.

MUM: Henry, we're having Aunt Ruby for lunch this Sunday.
HENRY: Can't we have roast beef instead?

MUM: Henry! Why did you put a slug in Aunt Ruby's bed?

HENRY: I couldn't find a snake.

AUNT RUBY: Goodness! It's raining cats and dogs.

HENRY: I know. I nearly stepped in a poodle.

AUNT RUBY: Well, Henry, I'm leaving tomorrow. Are you sorry?

HENRY: Oh yes, Aunt Ruby, I thought you were leaving today.

JOKES NOT TO TELL MISS BATTLE-AXE

These jokes are guaranteed to send teachers screaming from the classroom. Just don't blame me if you get sent to the Head . . .

What did the inflatable teacher say to the inflatable boy who brought a pin to the inflatable school?
You've let me down, you've let the school down, but worst of all, you've let yourself down.

MISS BATTLE-AXE: Henry! What is glue made out of?
HENRY: Um . . . sticks.

MISS BATTLE-AXE: Henry! Were you copying Susan's sums?
HENRY: No! I was just seeing if she'd got mine right.

HENRY: Would you blame someone for something they hadn't done?
MISS BATTLE-AXE: Of course not.
HENRY: Good, I haven't done my homework.

MISS BATTLE-AXE: Henry, I hope I didn't see you copying Clare.

HENRY: I hope you didn't either.

MISS BATTLE-AXE: Linda! Why are you late for school again?

LAZY LINDA: I overslept.

MISS BATTLE-AXE: You mean you sleep at home as well?

*What would
you get if you
crossed Miss
Battle-Axe with
a vampire?*
Lots of blood tests.

MISS BATTLE-AXE:
William! You've put
your shoes on the
wrong feet.

WEEPY WILLIAM: Waaaah! But
these are the only feet I've got.

MISS BATTLE-AXE: Henry! You missed
school yesterday, didn't you?

HENRY: Not very much.

MISS BATTLE-AXE: Henry! If you
multiplied 1497 by 371 what answer
would you get?

HENRY: The wrong one.

MISS BATTLE-AXE: Henry, where are the
Kings and Queens of England crowned?
HENRY: On their heads.

MISS BATTLE-AXE: Henry, make up a
sentence with the word 'lettuce' in it.
HENRY: Let us out of school early.

*What's the difference between homework and
an onion?*
Nobody cries when you cut up
homework.

MISS BATTLE-AXE: Henry! I'm sending you off the football pitch.

HENRY: What for?

MISS BATTLE-AXE: The rest of the match.

> **MISS BATTLE-AXE**: Henry, what is a mushroom?
>
> **HENRY**: The place where they make school dinners.

Did you hear about the cross-eyed teacher? He couldn't control his pupils.

MISS BATTLE-AXE: Henry! Why are you doing a headstand in the classroom?

HENRY: You said we should turn things over in our minds.

HENRY: I wish we lived in the olden days.

RALPH: Why?

HENRY: We wouldn't have so much history to learn.

MISS BATTLE-AXE: Henry, I do wish you'd pay a little attention.

HENRY: Believe me, I'm paying as little as I can.

Miss Battle-Axe: That's the most horrid boy in the whole school.

Mum: That's my son.

Miss Battle-Axe: Oh, I'm so sorry.

Mum: *You're* sorry?

PERFECT PETER'S FAVOURITE JOKES

'NO! I don't want Peter's stupid, smelly jokes in my joke book.'

'Don't be horrid, Henry!'

'I DON'T WANT PETER'S STUPID, BABY JOKES IN MY BOOK.

AND THAT'S FINAL.'

'Henry, I'm warning you . . .'

'NOOOOOOOO!'

'That's it, Henry. No TV for a week.'

'Oh all right. He can put in his stupid, yucky jokes.'

Psst. Listen, everyone, don't read them. They're awful. Skip ahead to the next section.

What's green and rides a horse?
Alexander the Grape.

**I thought I said, don't read
Peter's dumb jokes!**

What do you call a sheep on a trampoline?
A woolly jumper.

*What happens if you fall asleep under
a car?*
You wake up oily in the morning.

Told you they were awful! Now stop reading!

Why couldn't the sailor play cards?
The captain was standing on the deck.

How do chickens dance?
Chick to chick

Groan.

Why did the man with one hand cross the road?
To get to the second hand shop.

Why did the germ cross the microscope?
To get to the other slide.

What do you get if you dial 666?
The Australian police.

How do you use an Egyptian doorbell?
Just toot-and-come-in.

What's orange and sounds like a parrot?
A carrot.

*What do you get if you pour hot water
down a rabbit hole?*
Hot cross bunnies.

**You still here? Then it's your
own fault if you have to read
dumb bunny jokes.**

What do you call a blind reindeer?
No eye deer.

Why did the elephant cross the road?
The chicken was on holiday.

'Peter! That's my joke. I already told it.'

'It's my joke! You stole it.'

'Didn't.'

'Did.'

'MUMMMMMMMMMM!'

Why did the bubblegum cross the road?
It was stuck to the chicken's foot.

What do you call a man who's been buried in a bog for 4000 years?
Pete.

What do you call a priest on a motorbike?
Rev.

Where do frogs hang their coats?
In a croakroom.

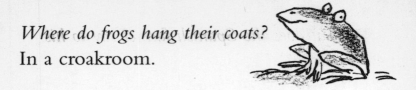

Peter! That's the worst joke I've ever heard. Cross it out this minute.

What did the policeman say to his belly?
'You're under a vest.'

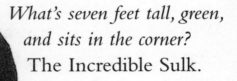

What's seven feet tall, green, and sits in the corner?
The Incredible Sulk.

What do you call a bear without an ear?
B.

Only an ugly, smelly toad would find that funny.

What does the Spanish farmer say to his chickens?
'Oh lay!'

What did the martian say to the petrol pump?
Take your finger out of your ear when I'm talking to you.

When is a tractor not a tractor?
When it turns into a field.

When I'm king, anyone who tells any of Peter's stupid jokes will get trampled on by elephants. I mean it!

How do you know flowers are lazy?
You always find them in beds.

What happens when you drop a green rock in the Red Sea?
It gets wet.

Aaarrrgghhh.

Which pet makes the most noise?
A trum-pet.

They're finished. Phew. That was horrible. I'm going to glue those pages together so no one will ever have to suffer again.

JOKES MUCH TOO RUDE TO TELL MUM

Yes! Now some real jokes.

What did the constipated mathematician do?
He got a pencil and worked it out.

What jumps out from behind a snowdrift and shows you his bottom?
The A–bum–inable snowman.

If a centipede a pint and a millipede a litre, how much can a precipice?

A little girl wet herself in class and the teacher asked her why she didn't put up her hand. 'I did, Miss, but it ran through my fingers.'

If you're American when you go into the toilet and American when you come out of the toilet, what are you when you're in the toilet?
European.

What did the doctor say to the man wearing cling-film?
'I can clearly see you're nuts.'

Knock Knock.
Who's there?
Madam.
Madam who?
Madam fingers
are stuck in
the keyhole!

Knock Knock!
Who's there?
Done up.
Done up who?
You did a poo?!

Did you hear about the cannibal who passed his cousin in the woods?

What did the elephant say to the naked man?
'You can't pick up —'

'Henry! That's enough! Go to your room!'